George Washington

First U.S. President

Colonial Leaders

Lord Baltimore *English Politician and Colonist*

Benjamin Banneker *American Mathematician and Astronomer*

William Bradford *Governor of Plymouth Colony*

Benjamin Franklin *American Statesman, Scientist, and Writer*

Anne Hutchinson *Religious Leader*

Cotton Mather *Author, Clergyman, and Scholar*

William Penn *Founder of Democracy*

John Smith *English Explorer and Colonist*

Miles Standish *Plymouth Colony Leader*

Peter Stuyvesant *Dutch Military Leader*

Revolutionary War Leaders

Benedict Arnold *Traitor to the Cause*

Nathan Hale *Revolutionary Hero*

Alexander Hamilton *First U.S. Secretary of the Treasury*

Patrick Henry *American Statesman and Speaker*

Thomas Jefferson *Author of the Declaration of Independence*

John Paul Jones *Father of the U.S. Navy*

Thomas Paine *Political Writer*

Paul Revere *American Patriot*

Betsy Ross *American Patriot*

George Washington *First U.S. President*

Revolutionary War Leaders

George Washington

First U.S. President

Tara Baukus Mello

Arthur M. Schlesinger, jr.
Senior Consulting Editor

Chelsea House Publishers

Philadelphia

Produced by 21st Century Publishing and Communications, Inc.
New York, NY. http://www.21cpc.com

CHELSEA HOUSE PUBLISHERS
Editor in Chief Stephen Reginald
Production Manager Pamela Loos
Director of Photography Judy L. Hasday
Art Director Sara Davis
Managing Editor James D. Gallagher

Staff for *GEORGE WASHINGTON*
Project Editor/Publishing Coordinator Jim McAvoy
Associate Art Director Takeshi Takahashi
Series Design Keith Trego

The Chelsea House World Wide Web address is
http://www.chelseahouse.com

First Printing
1 3 5 7 9 8 6 4 2

Library of Congress Cataloging-in-Publication Data

Mello, Tara Baukus.
George Washington / by Tara Baukus Mello.
80 pp. cm. — (Revolutionary War Leaders series)
Includes bibliographical references and index.
Summary: A biography of George Washington, the general who led
the American army in the Revolutionary War and then became the
first president of the United States.
ISBN 0–7910–5352–0 (hc)   ISBN 0–7910–5695–3 (pb)
1. Washington, George, 1732–1799—Juvenile literature. 2. Presidents—
United States—Biography—Juvenile literature. 3. Generals—United
States—Biography—Juvenile literature. 4. United States—History—
Revolution, 1775–1783—Biography Juvenile literature. [1. Washington,
George, 1732–1799. 2. Presidents.] I. Title. II. Series.
E312.66.M44   1999
973.4'092—dc21   99-23987
[B]   CIP

Publisher's Note: In Colonial and Revolutionary War America, there were no standard rules for spelling, punctuation, capitalization, or grammar. Some of the quotations that appear in the Colonial Leaders and Revolutionary War Leaders series come from original documents and letters written during this time in history. Original quotations reflect writing inconsistencies of the period.

Contents

George Washington grew up in Virginia on a tobacco plantation like this one. Most plantations were located along rivers so that ships could sail right up to the plantation, load up the tobacco, and carry it to Britain.

1

Growing Up

When George Washington was born on February 22, 1732, he was the fourth generation of his family to live in America. Around 1657, his great-grandfather John Washington came from England to live in America. John Washington settled on the edge of the Potomac River in Virginia, built his own tobacco **plantation**, and was involved in the local government. Virginia was an English colony at that time.

George's father, Augustine Washington, grew tobacco at a plantation called Ferry Farm and later at another plantation called Little Hunting Creek, along the banks of the Potomac River. Augustine Washington's plantations were spread over 10,000 acres, and 50 slaves helped maintain them. George and his brothers and sister lived with Augustine and Mary, their mother, in the four-room farmhouse where George was born.

When George was six years old, Lawrence, George's half brother, returned from school in England. Lawrence was 20 years old at the time, and the two became best friends immediately. When George was growing up, he wanted to be just like his brother, who was a member of the British Navy and had fought in battles between Britain and Spain. It seemed, however, that George was destined to be a tobacco planter like his father.

George's education began with a tutor whom his father hired when George was seven or eight years old. When he was a couple of years older, he went to a log schoolhouse in Fredericksburg, where he studied reading, mathematics, geography, surveying, and astronomy. Like his two older half brothers, Lawrence and Augustine, who was named after their father, George was supposed to go to the Appleby School in London, England, for a formal education when he got older.

In 1743 George's life changed. His father died, and his mother was left to manage the plantation and take care of the Washington children. Of the five younger children, George was the oldest. Even though he was just 11 years old, he was expected to take on many of his father's duties. Although George's father and half brothers had attended school in England, George and his younger siblings did not go. There was not enough money, and they needed to stay at home and help run Ferry Farm.

Although George stopped going to school when he was 15 years old, he worked hard at getting the education of an English gentleman. He read and copied passages from books to learn as much as he could and practiced his handwriting at the same time. George copied all the 110 rules from a book of **etiquette** called *Rules of Civility and Decent Behaviour in Company and Conversation*, which included not undressing in public.

When George was a teenager, Lawrence married a woman named Anne, who came from a very important Virginia family, the Fairfaxes. Lawrence inherited their father's plantation by the Potomac River, and later he renamed the plantation Mount Vernon after an English admiral whom he served under when he was in the British Navy. Lawrence and Anne lived at Mount Vernon, and George visited them whenever he could get away from his duties at Ferry Farm.

George enjoyed his time at Mount Vernon very much because he was able to spend lots of time with his best friend, Lawrence, and he got a glimpse into the **aristocracy** with the important Fairfax family. Lawrence watched out for his younger brother and, when George was 16, helped him get a job as a **surveyor** for Lord

George often visited the beautiful Virginia estate of Mount Vernon by the Potomac River where his half brother Lawrence lived.

Fairfax, who owned more than five million acres of land in the area.

This was the first time George got to travel west, and he thought the country was beautiful. For a month, he surveyed the land. During his journey, he rode his horse, slept on the ground, and hunted for his own food. He also had a few adventures, including an unexpected encounter with a rattlesnake and the challenge of crossing a swiftly moving river while riding his horse. George loved exploring the countryside, and a few years later bought some land in the Shenandoah Valley for himself.

George kept his job with Lord Fairfax for several years until Lawrence became ill with **tuberculosis**. Then he moved with Lawrence to Barbados, an island in the West Indies. They hoped that the warm weather there would help Lawrence to get better. While in Barbados, George caught smallpox, a disease similar to chicken pox, which many people died from during that time. Luckily, George survived, but he was left with some scars on his face from the scabs caused by the disease. Lawrence, however, never recovered and died in the summer of 1752.

Before Lawrence became sick, he had been the leader of the Virginia **militia**, which made him a very important man. Lawrence was also a member of the Ohio Company, a group of

Virginians who had joined together to get the rights to hundreds of thousands of acres of land in Ohio from King George II of England. Native Americans already lived there, however, and they wanted to protect their homes and hunting grounds. The French, Britain's biggest enemy, were also trying to take over the land in Ohio and were building forts on it.

George knew that it would be best for Britain to claim the land. He saw a great opportunity for the colonists to gain new territory. So he decided to try to get Lawrence's old job with the militia. Little did George know where this career in the military would take him.

Young George poses in his uniform as an officer in the Virginia militia. Although he did not have much military experience, he soon found himself leading militiamen to the western frontier to fight the French.

Early Career

Even though George was just 20 years old and did not have any experience in the military, he decided to try for his brother's job in the militia. Lawrence's job was divided into four separate positions, and George was given one of them. He was now a major in the Virginia militia. One of George's duties was to train the volunteer militia how to fight. Since George did not have any military experience, he tried to teach the volunteer militia the necessary skills from books he had read.

One of George's most dangerous assignments during this period was to travel to Lake Erie to deliver the message from the king of England to the French that the British were claiming land in Ohio. George and a few men marched west for more than a month. They had to travel through different Indian territories, including those of Britain's **allies**, the Iroquois tribe, and those of the "French Indians," the Native Americans who were France's allies. When George arrived at Lake Erie and delivered the king's message, the French officer told him that France was not going to cooperate with the British and that he should leave the region. George needed to get back to Virginia as quickly as possible. France's refusal to leave Ohio meant that there would soon be a war between the two nations.

When George took the momentous news back to Lieutenant Governor Dinwiddie of Virginia, Dinwiddie requested a written report of what happened. George wrote a detailed report that was about as long as this book. The report was later published in both America and London, and it made George famous to both the American people and to the British. George was promoted to the rank of lieutenant colonel.

At age 22, George was the second highest-ranking person of the Virginia **Regiment**. Soon, George and 160 men marched west toward a place called the Forks, where two rivers meet to form the Ohio River. When they arrived, they discovered that the French had already occupied the area and had built Fort Duquesne (pronounced du-kane). A small battle broke out. The shots that were fired in this battle at Great Meadows were the first shots of the French and Indian War, also called the Seven Year's War.

Although war was not officially declared until two years later, in 1754, it was already a war to the men who were fighting, including George. So he and his men built Fort Necessity, about 50 miles from the Forks in Ohio. It wasn't long before the French attacked Fort Necessity, and when they did, George's men fought for hours in the rain, trying to defend themselves and their

Rugged soldiers and their Native American allies confront the enemy in one of many battles that took place during the French and Indian War.

territory. They were greatly outnumbered, and the French were also much more experienced soldiers than the American and British men who were under George's command. Finally, George and his men surrendered, and the French allowed them to return to Virginia unharmed.

The battle was considered by many people to have been a disaster. The soldiers had not been prepared to fight. Their gunpowder was not protected from the rain, so the wet substance could not be fired. Although many people looked poorly on George because of the failure of this battle, others saw him as a hero because he fought bravely even when he was outnumbered.

Not long after this battle, George quit his position in the military. The Virginia Regiment had been divided up, and the British Army decided that the highest rank for a colonist would be captain. This was a big **demotion** for George. Rather than accept a lower position, he resigned.

In 1754 George went home. He rented Mount Vernon from Lawrence's **widow**, Anne, and hoped to get married and raise his own family there. George added a third story to the house to make room for his future children. He soon began growing tobacco, the crop that his **ancestors** had grown for so many generations.

Tobacco, however, was extremely hard on the soil and required the work of many people to maintain. Also it was sold primarily in Britain, which meant that tobacco farmers had to depend heavily on events that happened very far away to determine if they would be able to make enough money to pay their bills and support their families. Because of these problems, George began to look for new crops that he could grow to replace tobacco. He experimented with many different kinds of seeds and tried a very new technique for farming called crop rotation.

Crop rotation is moving the crops to a new location at the end of the season. It is a very common practice today. Each crop uses different parts of the soil, called nutrients, to stay healthy. The soil can get unbalanced by growing the same crop in the same location year after year. By rotating the crops, the soil can stay very healthy, making the crops grow better. George was one of the first farmers in America to try crop rotation.

The decision to change from one crop—tobacco—to many crops was very different from the way George's great-grandfather John had planted when he moved to Virginia. John was a *planter*, which meant that he relied on one crop to earn his living. When George began to invest in a variety of crops, including grains and vegetables, he became a *farmer*. His experiments with crop rotation and other farming techniques, such as plowing, were very important to him. He loved the experiments and, for the rest of his life, he would look for new ways to make the farms at Mount Vernon successful.

While George was farming at Mount Vernon, the fighting over the territory in Ohio had gotten much worse. Major General Edward Braddock, the leader of one of the regiments of the British Army, asked George to join him as a volunteer aide. George worked at the army's headquarters until the summer of 1755 when General Braddock decided to attack the French at Fort Duquesne. Although George had been sick for several weeks, he told General Braddock that he wanted to go along.

General Braddock set out with 1,500 men.

Most of the men were British soldiers, but some were colonists like George. George tried to warn the general that his army would not be able to fight the way they had been trained. The British were trained to fight in a big field in a line of soldiers called a formation. George knew that the French would not fight this way. The general did not take George's warning. The French attacked just a few miles from Fort Duquesne on July 9. Taken completely by surprise, almost all of the British soldiers were either killed or wounded by a few hundred French soldiers and their Native American allies.

During the fighting, George's horse was shot from under him, and he had to jump on another, which was also killed soon thereafter. Bullets ripped through George's coat, and his hat was shot off his head, but he was not injured. General Braddock, however, was severely wounded from a shot in the lungs. He ordered George to leave and get more soldiers who could help in the battle. George rode 40

George Washington receives orders from a fatally wounded General Braddock in the battle with the French not far from Fort Duquesne.

miles in the night to get the soldiers, but they were too scared to fight. The general died a few days later while George and what was left of the men retreated all the way to Philadelphia.

Once again, George was recognized for his courage and bravery during a battle, this time by both Virginia and Britain. Soon thereafter, Governor Dinwiddie named George commander of all of the Virginia troops. Now a colonel, George oversaw the troops for more than three years. It was a hard job. He and his men tried to protect many miles of territory. There were not enough supplies, weapons, or well-trained soldiers, and George complained about the situation to many people. Although he often told people he was going to resign, George never really gave up. When he was 26, and the French retreated, he fought what he believed to be his last battle. With the war over, George was sure there was no way his military career would move forward, so he finally resigned.

George went back to Mount Vernon. There he worked on his farm, went on foxhunts, and attended dances. He began to spend time with Martha Custis, a widow he had met at one of the dances. Martha was one of the wealthiest women in Virginia. She had inherited about 18,000 acres of land and 300 slaves from her husband when he died. George, who was a famous colonel by this time, now owned thousands of acres of land and 20 slaves. George and Martha liked each other very much. It wasn't very long before they got engaged, and on January 6, 1759, George and Martha were married. The marriage made them one of the most important families in all of Virginia.

Martha moved to Mount Vernon with her two young children from her first marriage. There were John Parke Custis, the four-year-old who was nicknamed "Jackie," and Martha Parke Custis, the two-year-old who was called "Patsy." George and Martha were a good match for each other. They had similar views about life and they enjoyed many of the same activities, such as horseback riding.

George became a member of the House of Burgesses in Virginia, the group of leaders who made decisions about Virginia's government.

Martha Custis, who had her own land and slaves, was a 27-year-old widow with two children when she married George.

But he mostly concentrated on spending time with his new family, traveling only when the House of Burgesses met in Williamsburg. George spent a lot of time with Jackie and little Patsy. He sent to London for toys and clothing for them and even ordered musical instruments for them to play. Patsy received a **spinet** and later Jackie was given a violin and a flute. George loved music and, although he could not sing or play an instrument, he loved to dance.

For 15 years, George managed his land at Mount Vernon, gradually replacing the tobacco with grains and other crops. George bought more slaves to help take care of his land. Most of these slaves were purchased right off the ships that had carried them from Africa. George treated his slaves better than many owners did. By 1770, George had gotten another 30,000 acres of land in what today is West Virginia.

These years were the happiest times George ever had. Farming was what he loved, even though most of his life was spent doing other things. George said, "[Farming] has been the most pleasing occupation of my life, and the most congenial to my temper, notwithstanding that a small proportion of it has been spent in this way."

As commander of the Continental Army, General George Washington reviews battle plans with his trusted officers. George had to gather an army of untrained civilians, teach them to fight, and lead them in a difficult war against the British.

Military Leader

3

By 1774, America was again having major difficulties. George left Mount Vernon and traveled to Philadelphia, Pennsylvania, to join the Continental Congress, a group of colonial leaders who wanted to make sure that the colonists' rights were protected. The Continental Congress decided that Britain did not have the right to tax them or to tell them how to run their own government. In addition, the group decided to **boycott** the trade of all goods with Britain. The British were not happy with America's new attitude toward them. They were ready to do whatever was necessary to make sure the colonies remained firmly under the control of, and continued to pay taxes to, the British government.

By the time the Continental Congress met for the second time in 1775, American and British soldiers had started fighting. In June of 1775 the Continental Congress chose George to head the Continental Army of the Revolutionary War and gave him the title of General. When George was appointed commander-in-chief of the army, there were no soldiers. It was up to George to recruit the colonists for service, build an army, and lead the fight.

Although George was a famous and brave soldier, he was not very happy about going back into war again. He told Martha, whom he also called Patsy, that he would much rather have stayed with her and the family at Mount Vernon. He wrote, "You may believe me, my dear Patsy, when I assure you in the most solemn manner that, so far from seeking this appointment, I have used every endeavor in my power to avoid it . . . " George also knew, however, that he could not say no, for if he did, it would seem as if he did not believe in America's independence.

On July 2, 1775, George arrived at the Continental Army's camp near Boston, Massachusetts, to take command. He worked hard to train the soldiers and struggled to make sure that they had food and supplies. Each winter, Martha went to the Continental Army's camp to be with George and then left in the spring when the men went off for battles. Although winter camp was relatively safe, there was still a war going on. About her first winter visit between 1775 and 1776, Martha wrote in a letter to a friend, "Some days we have a number of Cannon and shells from Boston and Bunkers Hill, but it does not seem to surprise any one but me; I confess I shudder every time I hear the sound of a gun."

On March 4, 1776, George and the newly formed Continental Army finally won their first victory. During the night, the army had brought cannons up to the top of a hill in Dorcester Heights near Boston. From there, the army could fire into the city and into the unsuspecting British camp. When General William Howe, who was in charge of the British forces, woke up the next morning, he saw what the colonists had done. Since it was too dangerous for the British to stay within the range of the cannons, they boarded ships and left Boston.

The colonists had been fighting with the British for a year, yet they were not really sure exactly what they were fighting for. Some colonists believed that they were fighting to be treated fairly by the British government. Others thought that they were fighting to form their own country, independent from British rule. As the fighting continued, more and more of the colonists began to believe in the fight for independence. Finally, as the Continental Army was anxiously awaiting battle on Long Island, in the

New York colony, the announcement came. Congress had voted for independence. It was now officially a war for freedom.

Within a few months, Thomas Jefferson, one of the members of Congress, began to write the Declaration of Independence. Once Benjamin Franklin and John Adams, who were also members of the Congress, offered their input, the document was sent for all members of Congress to review. After some additional revisions had been made, it was adopted by Congress on July 4, 1776, just as more British ships began arriving in the northeast. When George heard the news, he sent out orders to have the document read out loud to every unit in the Continental Army.

Enthusiastic colonists in New York celebrated the announcement of the Declaration of Independence by pulling down a cast-iron statue of Britain's King George III and sending the metal to Connecticut to be melted down and forged into bullets to fire at the British.

Within two weeks, more than 39,000 British soldiers arrived on 427 supply ships and 52 **man-of-war** ships. The superior British forces

With John Adams on his right and Benjamin Franklin at his left, Thomas Jefferson presents the Declaration of Independence to the Continental Congress.

soon took over New York and New Jersey. In August the British captured New York City, and when they headed toward the Continental Army, George ordered his army to retreat to

Pennsylvania. Each time the British struck, with their greater numbers and better training, they killed, wounded, or captured many of the American soldiers. Toward the end of 1776, the Continental Army had only 3,000 soldiers left, compared to the 15,000 men George had the year before. To make matters worse, most of the soldiers would be free to leave soon, since their enlistment period would expire on January 1, 1777.

George thought that the British would soon win the war. However, he had to try his best to fight because he believed that America should be free from the British. Late on Christmas night, he gathered most of his men in boats and led them across the Delaware River from Pennsylvania into New Jersey. The soldiers marched all night through the wind and sleet until they surprised the British forces at Trenton, New Jersey. After winning the battle at Trenton, George moved quickly to attack the British regiments in Princeton and won that battle too. These two victories gave the Americans a chance at winning the Revolutionary War.

Soon, more and more American colonists joined the Continental Army, since it seemed now there was a real chance of winning their freedom. The growing American forces won a significant victory at Saratoga, New York, in the fall of 1777, when they captured almost 6,000 British soldiers.

The armies stopped fighting for the bitter winter of 1777–1778 as the Americans camped near Valley Forge in Pennsylvania. For the first two months of the winter, the soldiers suffered awfully. There was not enough food, clothing, or other essential supplies. About one-quarter of George's men died from the cold weather, hunger, or disease. The horrible conditions upset George terribly. He wrote what he observed, "Men, without Clothes to cover their nakedness; without Blankets to lay on; without Shoes, by which their marches might be traced, by the Blood from their Feet."

George leads his troops to victory in the Battle of Trenton after making a daring nighttime attack on British forces.

By the spring of 1778, George learned that France had agreed to support the Americans in their war with Britain. The Continental Army now had a partner that had many soldiers and ships, which would make the war between

America and Britain more closely matched. The British retreated to New York City and the Continental Army camped on the outskirts of the city. For the next three years, most of the fighting took place in the South, where both the Americans and the British won and lost battles. Then, in 1781, Lord Cornwallis, the leader of the British army in the South, invaded Virginia and took over Yorktown.

Five thousand French soldiers, whose leader was General Jean Rochambeau, had met up with and joined George and his men. While George and Rochambeau were talking about attacking New York City, they received a message that the French Navy was on its way to help, but could not travel as far as New York. George and Rochambeau gave up on the idea of attacking New York right away. Instead they decided to attack Yorktown with the combined forces of the Continental and French armies from the land and the French Navy from the sea.

It was about 450 miles from the camp of the

George prays for his soldiers and for American victory during the terrible winter they endured at Valley Forge.

Continental and French armies to Yorktown. George knew that if the army had any hope of getting there without the British in New York City knowing, he had to have a good plan.

George intentionally let some British spies see what looked like secret documents that said the French Navy was sailing to New Jersey. Then, he had some men begin the preparations to build a new camp in New Jersey, one that would be big enough for many men. In the meantime, the Continental and French armies marched part of the way toward Yorktown and then took boats down the Delaware River the rest of the way. George rode his horse ahead of the men to make sure that the French Navy actually arrived.

Another important person in the Revolutionary War was the Marquis de Lafayette, who was also one of George's good friends. He was 20 years old when he came from France to help the colonists win the war and was given the high rank of major general.

On September 5, 1781 the Continental and French armies began to close in on the British in Yorktown, while at sea the French Navy fought the British fleet. Try as they might, the British ships were not able to get past the line of French ships to help Lord Cornwallis. On

**The Marquis de Lafayette was an ideal-
istic young French aristocrat who joined
up with the Continental Army and
fought several battles alongside George.**

October 17, the Continental and French armies
opened fire with all the weapons they had and
all their force of will. Lord Cornwallis and his

troops could not hold out any longer and called for a **truce**. On October 19, they surrendered.

Although this was the last major battle of the war for independence, the Continental Army stayed out in the field for another two miserable years. During this period, the men waited for the peace **treaty** to be signed by both Britain and America. George's men got more and more restless as time passed by, eager to get paid and go home to their families. George called a meeting to talk to his men and try to persuade them that they should be patient for a little while longer. The men, however, were not moved by his speech. In a final effort to convince them, George remembered the letter in his pocket from a certain congressman and decided to read it out loud.

When he opened the letter, he stared at it blankly. After a moment, he pulled out a pair of eyeglasses, something his men had never seen him wear before. He said to them, "Gentlemen, you must pardon me. I have grown gray in the service of my country and now find myself going blind." In that moment, many of the soldiers were so moved they broke down and cried. George's speech had been a success.

Three days later, on March 18, 1783, George received word that the treaty had been agreed to by both countries. In September, the British and the Americans signed the treaty and, once the British left New York City, George resigned his position as commander. On Christmas Eve, 1783, he rode his horse home to Mount Vernon, where he planned to spend the rest of his life as a retired gentleman working on his farm.

To the cheers of his greeters, George, who has just left his beloved Mount Vernon home in Virginia, arrives in New York City, the nation's first capital, to be inaugurated as the first president of the newly formed United States of America.

4

The First President

When George arrived home, he found that the eight years he had been away had been very hard on Mount Vernon. The many construction projects he had started had not been completed, and his farm was not doing very well. He quickly set about the task of turning Mount Vernon into the place he had dreamed about. George started remodeling the buildings again, and he personally oversaw the creation of a bowling green, where he and his guests could enjoy some outdoor recreation.

Although he had replaced his tobacco crops

with wheat many years before, George still felt his farming methods could be improved upon. Once again he began to learn about more farming techniques. This time his ideas came from some forward-thinking farmers back in England. Armed with his new ideas and concepts, George bought more good land around Mount Vernon to try them out. Mount Vernon now had five separate farms, each with many fields for different experimental farming techniques. George tried things like planting seeds in evenly spaced rows, an idea that was completely new to American farmers at that time.

George also tried to improve his farm animals. The king of Spain had given him a rare mule as a gift, which he bred with some of his horses to create a larger and stronger breed of mules to work on his farm. As a result of what George did, the United States today has a breed of very strong mules.

In addition to changes in methods of farming, there was another great change waiting to take place at Mount Vernon. George had begun to feel uncomfortable about having slaves and thought that people should not "own" other people. This idea was very unusual at the time, and people would have thought poorly of George if he shared these thoughts with others. In 1786 he wrote, "I never mean to possess another slave by purchase; it being among my first wishes to see some plan adopted, by which slavery in this Country may be abolished by slow, sure & imperceptible degrees."

In 1787 George decided to come out of retirement to oversee the Constitutional Convention, a meeting of a group of leaders who gathered to revise a document called the Articles of Confederation. This document was the first constitution of the 13 states and was used from 1781 to 1789. As the convention progressed, some of its members proposed creating one government that would oversee all of the states. The idea was radical, but other members thought it was a good one. The system they eventually designed

Speaking at the Constitutional Convention only once, George works to persuade members to adopt a constitution for the new nation.

is the one we use today. Next, the group decided to have each state form a special convention to **ratify** the document.

By June 1788, nine states had ratified, and there were enough votes to put the Constitution in operation. Early in 1789, state officials, called electors, placed their votes to decide the president and vice president, according to the new process in the Constitution. In this first election, only 10 of the 13 states voted, but everyone who voted chose George as the president. John Adams had the second highest number of votes, so he became vice president. Although everyone knew that George would be their new leader, it was not official until the votes had been counted.

George waited at Mount Vernon to get the official news that he had been elected. He made preparations for construction on the buildings and for farming at Mount Vernon to continue while he went away to take over his new job. He even packed his bags so he would be ready to go as soon as he heard the news. Weeks passed and George continued to wait, all the time worrying that he would not be able to live up to everyone's expectations as the first president of the new nation. On April 14, 1789, Charles Thompson arrived at Mount Vernon on horseback. He carried with him a letter from the leader of the newly formed Senate which said George was officially the president of the United States of America.

George met Mr. Thompson in the large dining room, which he often called the "new room." This room is one of the most formal rooms at Mount Vernon and is where George and Martha often entertained guests. It was painted two shades of green and had fancy white decorations on the walls. Although the Washingtons called this room a dining room, they also used it for other purposes. Because of this, they brought in tables to eat at only when they needed them.

Two days after Mr. Thompson arrived with the news, George and an aide named David Humphreys left with Mr. Thompson for New York City, where George would live as the president. They traveled for eight days, stopping many times so George could make speeches and lead parades in his honor. When he arrived in New York City, there was a huge celebration. As a barge took him across the Hudson River, other ships fired 13-gun salutes. From there,

George was escorted in a parade to his new home. The streets of the route were lined with well-wishers, who waved their handkerchiefs and threw flowers. George was so moved by all the people that he had to wipe tears from his eyes.

One week later was George's **inauguration**. He rode a short distance in a carriage from his new house to Federal Hall. There he stood on the balcony of the building and took his oath of office. George wore a dark-brown suit, white silk stockings, and black shoes with silver buckles. He carried his sword at his side and had his hair powdered white and tied in the back, which was the custom at the time. After George had finished giving his inauguration speech, there was a religious service at a nearby chapel. At the end of the service, George went home to rest and to prepare for his first official day of work as president.

The work of the new government was not easy. Because the Constitutional Convention only outlined the role of the government, Congress had to make many decisions about exactly how things would work. George worked with Congress and the Senate to determine the departments of government and to make new policies. Soon, two political parties began to develop. The first were the Federalists, which were led by Alexander Hamilton, and later became the Republican Party, which we know today. The second were the Jeffersonian Democratic-Republicans, led by Thomas Jefferson, which is today's Democratic Party.

George oversaw all the aspects of the new government. For each department, George worked closely with the man he appointed to oversee it. Before making any important decisions, each department head met with the new president to get his approval. Many times George had breakfast with these men at which they talked until they could work out the best solution to the problem at hand.

Martha managed the president's house in

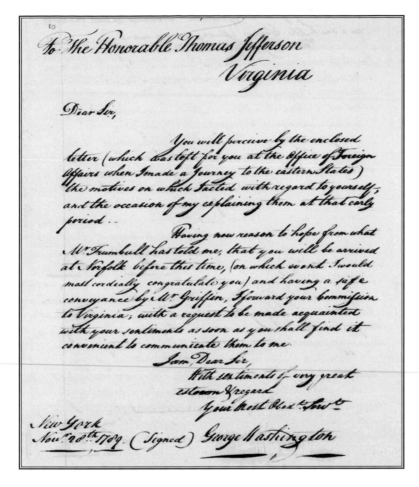

In 1789, George wrote this letter to Thomas Jefferson, whom he had appointed as the nation's first secretary of state.

New York City and later in Philadelphia when they moved there. She oversaw the staff and all the social functions for George. There were many tea parties, dances, and informal gatherings.

Thomas Jefferson became the leader of one of the nation's first political parties, the Democratic-Republicans.

There were also formal dinners, at which there were many courses with lots of different types of food. One guest was served apple pie, pudding, ice cream, and a variety of fruits and nuts for dessert, all in one evening.

George also began his ambitious plans for the new capital city. Washington, District of Columbia, would be located just a few miles from Mount Vernon. Heavily involved in the construction, George stopped to view the city's progress each time he traveled north or south. Ironically, George is the only president who did not live there.

In May 1792, George decided that he would resign at the end of his term. At age 60, George felt pretty old. His hearing was getting worse and his teeth had almost all fallen out. He thought that some-one younger would be bet-ter suited for the job, but James Madison, Thomas Jefferson, and Alexander

Many people still think that George had false teeth made of wood. George never had a set of teeth made of wood, but he did have some made of hippopotamus ivory. Getting false teeth to fit well was very difficult in those days and wearing them was uncomfortable. This is why some people think George looks uncomfortable in many of his portraits.

Hamilton changed his mind. They told him the country needed him and he decided to stay.

For five more years, George remained in service to his country as president, and these were probably the most unhappy years of his life. The two political parties were not getting along well and George was stuck in the middle. The politicians and newspapermen criticized George for his political decisions and even the way he acted in public. Early in 1796, George decided he was retiring at the end of his term in 1797 no matter what. He had had enough and wanted to go home to Mount Vernon where he could live the rest of his life in peace. With Alexander Hamilton's help, he revised the speech that had been prepared a few years earlier. To make it official, his Farewell Address was printed in a Philadelphia newspaper on September 19, 1796.

Many people thought George should remain as president of the United States of America until he died. George thought this idea would

The construction of the nation's new capital city, Washington, was begun when George was president but was not finished in time for him to live there.

make the position of the president too similar to that of Britain's king. Instead, George insisted that he retire after two terms, or eight years total. He also said that the new president should be elected by a vote. Every president thereafter

George bids a tearful goodbye to fellow officers.
His farewell to the nation as president was printed
in the newspapers.

followed George's wishes concerning two terms until Franklin Delano Roosevelt became president in the 1930s. President Roosevelt was actually elected to four terms but only served 12 years as president because he died while in office. In 1951, the Constitution was changed so that a president could only stay in office for two terms.

George's vice president, John Adams, was elected president on March 4, 1797, and George turned over the presidency to him. It is thought that this day was one of the happiest days of George's life.

George's fondest wish came true when he
retired to Mount Vernon to become once again
a peaceful farmer. He was tireless in inspecting
all aspects of his plantation, as he is here talking with an overseer during the harvest.

Peaceful Farmer

At age 65, George was finally able to lead the life he had always wanted—a farmer's life with days spent riding horses and overseeing the crops and animals. After a formal dinner in his honor, the retired first president happily went home. Unfortunately, in the eight years that George had been away, Mount Vernon had gotten pretty run down again. Just as when he had returned from the Revolutionary War, George discovered his buildings and lands were in sad shape. While he was president, he had sent many letters with specific instructions to the men who oversaw his farms at

Mount Vernon, but obviously his instructions had not been carried out effectively.

George's first job after he returned home was to put Mount Vernon back in order. He started work every day at sunrise and had breakfast with Martha and the rest of the household at seven o'clock. As was common at this time in Virginia, cold and boiled meats as well as tea and coffee were served. In addition, George often feasted on his favorite breakfast of three mush cakes soaked with butter and honey and three cups of tea without cream.

Almost every day, George took one of his many horses out to inspect different parts of his property. He rode about 20 miles each day, checking on the progress of the various crops, animals, gardens, and buildings. Each Saturday, the men who oversaw each of his farms and the different work crews gave George a report. Martha did not have as much energy as George, for her health had not been as good as his. The daily duties of running the household were now difficult for her, and she often spent her time copying letters that George had written.

George came in from his day's work for dinner, usually around three in the afternoon. This was the Washingtons' biggest meal of the day. Dinner was always lavish, with several different meats, a selection of vegetables, and lots of different desserts. George and Martha often had guests for dinner, rarely having a meal with just the two of them. George usually sat at the table after dinner for more than an hour, talking with his guests. At six in the evening, tea was served. Supper, a light meal, was sometimes served around nine o'clock, and other times not at all.

Cato was the name of George's favorite play. The play was about a Roman statesman who sacrificed everything for the good of his country. George often quoted lines from the play in his letters. He even had the play performed for his men when they were at Valley Forge.

In the summer of 1799, George decided to write a will. He was 66 years old and had already lived many years past the typical man's life span of that time. His eyesight and hearing had gotten even worse, and now his memory was affected too. In the will, he made sure that Martha would have what she needed. He also left portions of his estate to his nieces, nephews, and many of Martha's relatives. (Sadly, both Jackie and Patsy had already died.) In preparation for his will, George assessed all of his land, money, and other property, which amounted to $530,000. While this amount may not seem like a lot today, this made George one of the richest men in America at that time.

Part of the property that George assessed in his will were his slaves. When George counted them on that summer day, there were 314 slaves at Mount Vernon. George owned 125 of them and Martha owned the rest. Of the total, 132 were either too sick or too old to work.

Many of the adult slaves were married to each other and most of the child slaves had both their mothers and fathers living at Mount Vernon with them. Many of the slaves were

George and Martha were gracious hosts as they entertained friends and family at Mount Vernon after George's retirement.

trained in a trade and had skilled jobs on the farm such as blacksmith, painter, shoemaker, and gardener. Other slaves managed and over- saw the ongoing farm activities and gave their weekly reports to George. At this time slaves were not usually treated with much respect or given any responsibility, making George's actions very uncommon. Probably the kindest thing George ever did for his slaves, however, happened after he died. In his will, George said he wanted all the slaves he owned, upon Martha's death, to be freed. In addition, he said that he wanted the child slaves to be taught how to read and write. Adult slaves that were too old or too sick to work would be given money each year from the Washington family to help them live on their own.

On December 12, 1799, George went out for his daily horseback ride to inspect his property. It was cold and snowing, and when he returned his hair and clothes were wet from the snow. The next day George said his throat was sore. When he woke up in the middle of the night, he could hardly breathe. Three doctors were called. They gave George some different medicines and bled him, a process that was thought to cure people of illnesses at the time. Nothing worked. George knew he was near death. On December 14, at about 10:30 in the evening, George died.

The funeral was a few days later on the Mount Vernon grounds. George's coffin was carried from his house in a military procession down to the river. His friends walked between the lines of soldiers while guns were fired in salute. Martha watched from a window in their house while George was buried in the family tomb.

The citizens of the new country were greatly saddened by George's death. There were funeral parades and ceremonies in 300 cities and towns all across the nation. Military officers and citizens wore black clothing for months. Others bought small funeral medals and mourning rings to wear.

As the months passed, many people started naming buildings in George's memory. Dishes and other "souvenirs" of the first president were sold to many citizens. Books about his life began to appear. One of the best-selling books was published in 1800 by Parson Mason Locke Weems. *The Life and Memorable Actions of George Washington* was a book about George's life, but a lot of it was not true.

One story, about George chopping down a cherry tree when he was a little boy, was completely made up. Mr. Weems wrote that when George was six, his father found a cherry tree chopped down in their garden. When he asked George who had done it, George honestly admitted he had. The book was so popular that it was printed 80 different times and read by so many people that everyone began to think the cherry tree story was true.

Many of the things named after George Washington are very big and can still be seen today. For example, Mount Washington in New Hampshire is the tallest mountain in the northeastern U.S., standing at 6,288 feet. It was named by some climbers in 1784 who were studying the plants and trees on the mountain. Washington State, which was named for

George shares Mount Rushmore with three other great presidents–Thomas Jefferson, Abraham Lincoln, and Theodore Roosevelt.

George, became the 42nd state in 1889. Mount Rushmore in South Dakota, a giant monument to George and three other presidents, displays their faces carved into the side of a mountain.

Plans for the city of Washington, District of Columbia, began in 1791 and were overseen by George himself. The city's architect, Pierre L'Enfant, a famous French architect, designed the city to have many European elements, including an area called the Mall. The Mall, a wide and long street, would be surrounded by public buildings.

Although the nation's capital was named after George, it is the Washington Monument that was built in his memory. Construction of the monument began in 1848, but was not completed until 1884. The building is 555 feet tall and is made of more than 36,000 blocks of marble and granite. The pyramid at the very top is made out of aluminum and acts as a lightning rod. An elevator takes visitors almost to the top, where they can see Washington's entire great city below.

Mount Vernon is operated by the Mount Vernon Ladies' Association, which maintains and cares for much of the furniture, books, and other belongings of the Washingtons. The house, gardens, and crops have been completely restored using George's letters and journals as a guide. Each year more than one million visitors come to Mount Vernon to see the place where the father of our country lived and died.

GLOSSARY

allies–countries or groups that agree to support one another when they are in need.

ancestors–the relatives of a person who are older than the grandparents.

aristocracy–the upper class or nobility in a society.

boycott–to refuse to be associated with a certain group as a way to express disapproval of the group or its actions.

demotion–reducing a person's job title or military rank.

etiquette–rules for behaving well socially.

inauguration–a ceremony to admit a person into government office.

man-of-war–a type of ship used for combat.

militia–a group of civilian men called into the military only during emergencies.

plantation–an estate that harvests one crop on its land.

ratify–the process a group uses to approve a document.

regiment–a unit in an army.

spinet–a musical instrument with a keyboard and strings.

surveyor–a person whose job is to measure the land.

treaty–a document that outlines an agreement between two groups.

truce–an agreement between two groups to stop fighting.

tuberculosis–a serious disease of the lungs that often caused death during Washington's time.

widow–a woman who has not remarried after her husband's death.

CHRONOLOGY

1732   George Washington is born on February 22 in Virginia.

1743   George's father, Augustine, dies.

1748   Takes his first job as a surveyor for Lord Fairfax.

1751   Moves to Barbados with his half brother Lawrence and Lawrence's wife, Anne.

1752   Begins his military career.

1759   Marries Martha Dandridge Custis.

1775   Is named commander of the Continental Army; the Revolutionary War begins.

1781   British commander Lord Cornwallis surrenders to George at Yorktown, Virginia, the last battle of the war.

1789   Is elected the first president of the United States; moves to the then new capitol, New York City, with Martha.

1792   Plans to resign from presidency but is convinced to stay.

1797   Retires as president and moves back to Mount Vernon.

1799   Dies at Mount Vernon on December 14.

REVOLUTIONARY WAR TIME LINE

1765 The Stamp Act is passed by the British. Violent protests against it break out in the colonies.

1766 Britain ends the Stamp Act.

1767 Britain passes a law that taxes glass, painter's lead, paper, and tea in the colonies.

1770 Five colonists are killed by British soldiers in the Boston Massacre.

1773 People are angry about the taxes on tea. They throw boxes of tea from ships in Boston harbor into the water. It ruins the tea. The event is called the Boston Tea Party.

1774 The British pass laws to punish Boston for the Boston Tea Party. They close Boston harbor. Leaders in the colonies meet to plan a response to these actions.

1775 The battles of Lexington and Concord begin the American Revolution.

1776 The Declaration of Independence is signed. France and Spain give money to help the Americans fight Britain. Nathan Hale is captured by the British. He is charged with being a spy and is executed.

1777 Leaders choose a flag for America. The American troops win some important battles over the British. General Washington and his troops spend a very cold, hungry winter in Valley Forge.

1778 France sends ships to help the Americans win the war. The British are forced to leave Philadelphia.

1779 French ships head back to France. The French support the Americans in other ways.

1780 Americans discover that Benedict Arnold is a traitor. He escapes to the British. Major battles take place in North and South Carolina.

1781 The British surrender at Yorktown.

1783 A peace treaty is signed in France. British troops leave New York.

1787 The U.S. Constitution is written. Delaware becomes the first state in the Union.

1789 George Washington becomes the first president. John Adams is vice president.

FURTHER READING

Carter, Alden R. *The American Revolution*. New York: Franklin Watts, 1993.

Faber, Doris, and Harold Faber. *The Birth of a Nation*. New York: Charles Scribner's Sons, 1989.

Gilslin, James Cross. *George Washington: A Picture Book Biography*. New York: Scholastic, 1992.

Gross, Ruth Belov. *If You Grew Up with George Washington*. New York: Scholastic, 1993.

Heilbroner, Joan. *Meet George Washington*. New York: Random House, 1989.

Parin D'Aulaire, Ingri and Edgar. *George Washington*. New York: Doubleday, 1996.

Jaffe, Steven H. *Who Were the Founding Fathers?* New York: Henry Holt, 1996.

Reef, Catherine. *Mount Vernon*. New York: Dillon Press, 1992.

Woodruff, Elvira. *George Washington's Socks*. New York: Scholastic, 1993.

INDEX